Church Is Stranger Than Fiction

mary chambers

INTERVARSITY PRESS
DOWNERS GROVE, ILLINOIS 60515

InterVarsity Press is the book-publishing division of InterVarsity Christian Fellowship, a student movement active on campus at hundreds of universities, colleges and schools of nursing in the United States of America, and a member movement of the International Fellowship of Evangelical Students. For information about local and regional activities, write Public Relations Dept., InterVarsity Christian Fellowship, 6400 Schroeder Rd., P.O. Box 7895, Madison, WI 53707-7895.

Distributed in Canada through InterVarsity Press, 860 Denison St., Unit 3, Markham, Ontario L3R 4H1, Canada.

Cartoons on pages 5, 15, 65 and 67 used by permission of Leadership.

Cover illustration: Mary Chambers

ISBN 0-8308-1326-8

Printed in the United States of America

Library of Congress Cataloging-in-Publication Data

Chambers, Mary.
    Church is stranger than fiction/Mary Chambers.
       p.   cm.
    ISBN 0-8308-1326-8
     1. American wit and humor, Pictorial.   I. Title.
  NC1429.C457A4 1990   90-37194
                                    CIP

16   15   14   13   12   11   10   9   8   7   6   5   4   3   2   1
99   98   97   96   95   94   93   92   91   90

To my dad, Boyce Mouton, who got me started in cartooning,
and
my mom, Betty—now she knows what I've been doing instead of cleaning house.

Introduction

I love to look through photo albums. It's fun to try to figure out who is whom. It's also a real crowd-pleaser to point out pyramid bell-bottoms, double-knit Western wear, bouffant hairstyles and six-inch sideburns. However, I have to admit a certain sense of elation at the knowledge that there is no photographic evidence linking me with a certain red Naugahyde miniskirt, matching fringed vest and white go-go boots that I thought looked groovy at one time.

Pictures can show progress. A picture may remind you of just how bad the house looked before remodeling or of planting a little sapling that is now a tree that takes up most of the backyard. Cartoons can be like that as well.

Try to find yourself or your church in these cartoons. See if you remember things the way I do. Maybe you'll even recognize yourself "wearing" attitudes that don't complement you as much as you thought they did. Or, maybe you'll just recall the funny "saints" you've known and the good times you've had. After all, church *is* stranger than fiction.

Geraldo Rivera enters Christian broadcasting.

Four days? Boy! Time sure flies when you're dead!

I told him we didn't have the people. I told him we didn't have the budget . . .
but he just *had* to do a living Christmas tree.

Pastor Greer's attempt to raise his youth group's consciousness of Third World poverty was not entirely successful.

Roadcup, you've got a lot to learn about christening babies!

And is your husband working now . . . or is he still in the ministry?

I'm getting so old that all my friends in heaven will think I didn't make it.

Sidney tells me that your son doesn't close his eyes during the prayer.

After 27 years in the ministry it was bound to happen—he OD'd on fried chicken.

"Well, we call it *evandal*ism."

Tuesday morning . . . ladies' aerobics.

Yeah, I knew I was going to receive a real blessing the minute I saw his picture on the album cover.

How come when the pastor does it you call it "motivating" and when I do it you call it "nagging"?

By the way, did you notice that I added a little extra water softener to the baptistry this week?

This isn't so bad . . . last year I was Mary's donkey.

I'm sorry, Rev. Greer, sir, but the board just vetoed your proposal to increase defense spending.

... and when the pastor cut down the beanstalk, the giant committee came tumbling down and the church lived happily ever after ...

No, ma'am, I'm not a preacher. I've just been ill for a few days.

Can you imagine? A minister's wife who can't sing the third verse of "A Mighty Fortress Is Our God" without the hymnal!

Our bylaws specifically state that the will of God cannot be overturned without a 2/3 majority vote.

Now where exactly are you in the grief cycle?

It may say "yes" in the English, but in Greek that means "no"!

Here we have our "miracle parking spot"! Four out of five people who park here are healed before their feet hit the pavement!

. . . and a special word of thanks to those of you who helped with our Vacation Bible School.

. . . and I got that scar from the chairman of the Ladies' Aid Society during the second battle of "Guitars in the Sanctuary" back in '71.

We out of Static-Guard again, Roy?

. . . and we found this near the top of Mt. Ararat.

In the past 20 years here I feel I've come to know most of you pretty well . . .

cfiambers

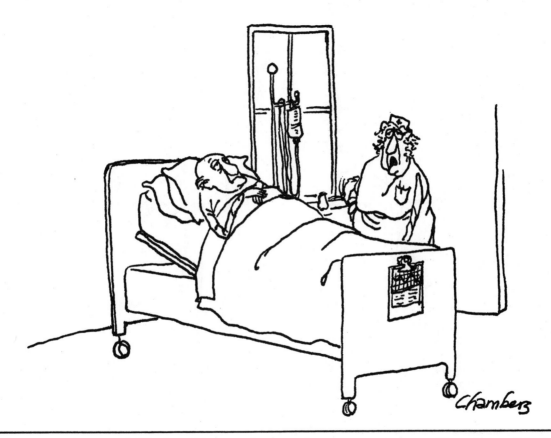

Good news, Reverend. The board has voted to pray for your recovery. . . . The vote was 5 to 4.

And why doesn't your teacher wash before he eats? Was he born in a barn?

We interrupt this sermon to inform you that the fourth-grade boys have taken over and are now in complete control of their classroom and are holding Miss McPeak hostage.

It's amazing how Rev. Clevenger manages to work the slides of his summer vacation into the Christmas program each year.

That was some sermon, Honey! The man across the aisle from me was in tears!

That was my old hermeneutics teacher!

. . . There being no other new business, the meeting was adjourned to the parking lot where members said what they really meant.

I've asked Peter to give each of you a copy of this week's discussion questions.

All right! So they made you chairman of the board . . . but don't you think you're carrying this a bit far?

I think my wife's first husband may have been an exception . . .

Pssst! Wind this up—there's a man from *Guinness Book of World Records* on the phone.

This one's called the "My-wife-can't-stand-the-parsonage blues."

... and the longer you hold them under, the more apt they are to be making real decisions ...

Now this little model is special-made for committees . . . it comes equipped with one gas pedal, four steering wheels and ten sets of brakes.

. . . And if the dead in Christ *do* rise first, this congregation's going to be with the Lord a good half hour before anybody else!

All right, how was the meeting, *really?*

So . . . what do *you* think is the most discouraging thing about the church?

You *are* coming to church this morning, aren't you?

OPTIMISTS FOR TODAY

Set up *all* the folding chairs for Wednesday night Bible study!

Made plans to meet his wife at 8:45 after an 8 o'clock board meeting!

Put her shoes back on when the minister said, ". . . in conclusion . . ."!

Well, I haven't actually *died* to sin, but I did feel kind of faint once!

It sure is sweet of you to help me with this permanent, Honey. I was afraid you might be mad about me criticizing your husband's preaching last week.

He's not counting Wednesday nights!

So if you aren't still mad, why do you keep whistling "God will take care of you"?

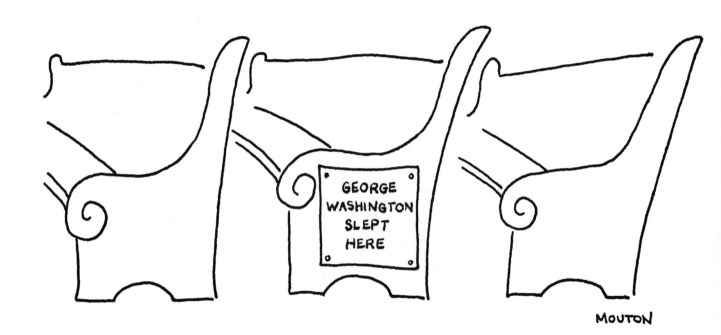

And now, in accordance with FCC regulations, we present the Republican version
of the Triumphal Entry . . .

It looks like we're going to have to recall our last 25 converts—there seems to be a defect in their giving.

I think our church is on the verge of renewal—they wanted to sing the third verse of a hymn last Sunday!

Baaaahrrrrriiimmmsstone-uh!

No, Mrs. Giovanni, my husband isn't home, but if it's counsel you're after, I've got a bit of advice!

I think the difference between men and women is that men have pie suppers
and women have salad luncheons.

chambers

Our visiting minister is speaking on "How a Christian Overcomes Fear."

You may have guessed I intend to address a controversial issue in the church today.

I told Bea I'd watch the nursery while she went to the restroom . . . let's see . . . that was 37 years ago . . .

You can quit smiling now, dear—we're home.

I had it done for Youth Emphasis Week!

And the big prize in the state lottery remains unclaimed till the winner, Rev. Marcum, finds the perfect disguise.

There's got to be an easier way to build a youth group!

We are pleased to announce that in spite of our reduced budget, we were still able
to afford a church organist.

That stupid marriage counsellor charged us $300—and that was just for an estimate!

This song isn't really special to me, but it does provide a wonderful showcase for my voice.

Have you ever stopped to consider how much more effective my sermons would be
if you weren't always yelling "HA!"?

Remember back when we were young and the difference between the clergy and the laity was none of the clergy were women?

Many churches are going to this heavy-duty model to protect their Sunday-school chalk.

Rev. Roadcup has finally found a friend to whom he can bare his soul.

It was perfect! Absolutely perfect! Why didn't we think to hire midgets before?

Oh, I could never divorce William. . . . Why, he's like one of the family.

So . . . what do you do the rest of the week? You got a job or something?

Rev. Greer refuses to negotiate. . . . He said we should talk to his agent.

Congratulations, Rev. Putnam. Your program to mobilize the laity was so successful we don't even need you anymore!

Oh, it's no bother. We love to have company drop in.

Based on early reports from two ushers and the church treasurer, we are projecting this morning's offering to be $5,917.02.

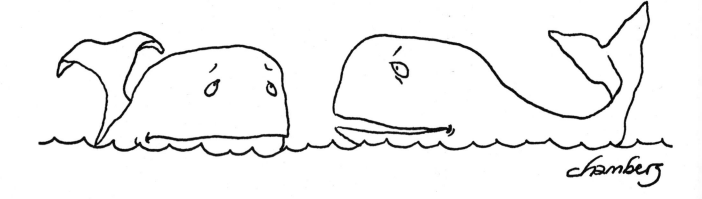

Oh sure! God told you to swallow him. I hope it makes you sick!

. . . and I'm sure our speaker today has spent many hours in prayer and preparation
for the message God has placed upon his heart . . .

Hi, Honey! I'm home from camp and just wait till I show you what I learned
watching the kids at campfire!

I think the deaf interpreter is ad-libbing again.

We go to the generic church . . . the tithe is only 9%.

Dear Grandma,
   Thank you for the tape recorder you sent for Christmas. I have already made quite a bit of money selling Dad tapes I've made around the house on Sunday mornings. I am saving up to buy a video camera.
   Thank you again.

   Love,
   Eldon

chambers

Oh, good . . . you're not busy.

It's my latest invention! This offering plate will ring a little bell if you put in $20 . . . if you don't put in anything, it takes your picture.

. . . and we'd sure appreciate it if whoever took the baptismal robes home to wash would bring them back . . .

Our congregation is so small that when the minister says "dearly beloved," I get embarrassed.

CLASSIFIED ADS

WANTED! CHURCH SECRETARY – Must be overweight, aged and surly. Apply for interview with pastor's wife. 358-5503

chambers

Solomon tells me I'm one in a thousand!

Sir, you have been recommended for our remedial singing class that meets in the basement of our annex.

It's 9:04 A.M. and Celia Miller decides that this Sunday *she's* going to sit in the car and honk.

As we sing the 314th verse of "Just as I Am," isn't there *ONE MORE* who will come?